The Serial Killer Handbook

◆ ◆ ◆

Facts That Are Stranger Than
Fiction

J. R. Mayfield

First published 2018 by Clikapedia LTD

ISBN 9781982983840

For Stacy

Without you this would not be possible

Also by J R Mayfield

The Ones Who Got Away
America's Serial Killers

I didn't want to hurt them. I only wanted to kill them.

- Sam Berkowitz

Table of Contents

Table of Contents

Intro

" I know I have to be destroyed. I was a mistake of nature.

- Andrei Chikatilo

"

Intro

The Serial Killer Handbook

What constitutes serial murder? The definition as given by the FBI's behavioural analysis unit is as follows:

Serial Murder: The unlawful killing of two or more victims by the same offender(s), in separate events.

This is as short and uncomplicated an answer as you can possibly get, as there isn't really a "one size fits all" box you can put a serial killer in. Most definitions of a serial killer revolve around an individual (or individuals) who kill two or more people (the number varies dependant on whom you ask) with a 'cooling off' period. The 'cooling off' period is one of the most important factors in distinguishing a serial killer from the likes of mass murderers and spree killers.

A serial killer can have a number of motives, though these can usually be placed into one of four categories.

Visionary, mission-oriented, hedonistic and power/control.

Visionary

The visionary killer usually believes they are being 'controlled' or otherwise coerced, usually by voices in their head, but also things such as visions. David Berkowitz (A.K.A The Son of Sam) believed a demon (or dog, depending on which story you believe) was telling him to kill, and so he did. This would put him in the category of a visionary serial killer.

Mission-oriented

The mission-oriented killer usually feels that it is his duty to rid the world of his victims, quite often targeting a certain group of people. Peter Sutcliffe claimed to be on a "mission" to "bump off" prostitutes, targeting the lone group would place him in the category of a mission-oriented serial killer.

Hedonistic

The hedonistic killer finds pleasure in causing pain, fear and death. Hedonistic serial killers can usually be placed into three sub-categories: lust, thrill and comfort. Jeffrey Dahmer would rape his victims after drugging them, and several times posthumously. He would also strangle most of his victims, as hedonistic killers need to feel close to the victim, a gun, for instance, would seem too impersonal. He would also go on to keep body parts such as genitals and would cannibalise some of the victims.

Power/control

The Power/control serial killer is motivated by having full control over their victim's life and death. They are usually highly organised and predatory. A large portion like to prolong the process, usually torturing the victim before the murder. Power/control killers also often rape the victim and/or engage in necrophilia after the murder, but unlike lust killers, this is not the main motive and is just another way for the killer to feel empowered and in total control. Dennis Rader is a prime example of a power/control killer. He would stalk his victim extensively, sometimes for years, before making his move. He would know their every move and have the entire process planned out beforehand. He would then commit the act with near precision and total disregard for any life other than his own.

So now we know the general profile of a serial killer. However, a general profile isn't what you came here for. So let's take a look outside of 'general', let's take a look outside of what can be labelled and categorized. Let's take a look at some of the awful things these monsters have actually done, some of the unthinkable acts these killers have committed, things that could not have been predicted, things the FBI's behavioural analysis unit could not teach, things that beg belief.

Within this book you will find the unbelievable facts behind some of the most unthinkable acts ever committed.

Random Fact

Richard Angelo had already been an eagle scout and a volunteer fireman before he graduated from university and became a nurse, so he was already used to helping others and saving lives. Though it seems the need to feel heroic was an unhealthy obsession. Working in the intensive care unit it wasn't uncommon for patients to pass away regularly, but the numbers seemed to increase during the graveyard shift whilst Angelo was working. It just so happened that Angelo's obsessive need to be the hero was not being met, and in order to feed it, he began injecting patients with Pavulon and Anectine in order to cause a near death state. He could then rush in and save their lives and everybody would see him as the hero he is. Unfortunately, he rarely saved a life, and by the time he was caught he had already killed 25 patients in search of glory.

Rodney Alcala

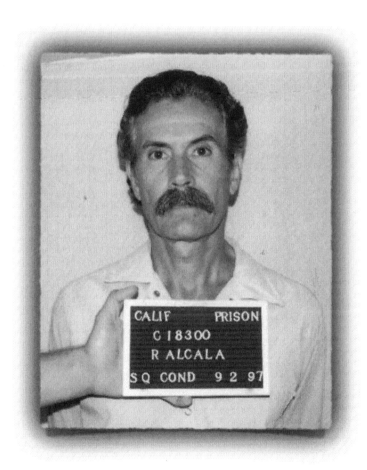

> **"** *I wanna kill, I wanna kill, I wanna see blood and gore and guts and veins in my teeth. Eat dead burnt bodies. I mean, kill, kill, kill, kill.*
>
> - Arlo Guthrie **"**

*This is part of a song Rodney Alcala played to the jury in court

Serial Killer Profile

Name: ———— Rodrigo Jacques Alcala Buquor

Nickname: ———— The Dating Game Killer

DOB: ———— 08/23/43

Country: ———— USA

Convicted murders: ———— 8

Estimated murders: ———— 130

Killing spree: ———— '71-'79

Caught: ———— 07/24/79

Modus operandi: ———— Varied/Strangulation

Victim profile: ———— Young Women

Sentence: ———— Death

Present: ———— California State Prison

Rodney Alcala

The Dating Game Killer

Rodney Alcala, also known as "The Dating Game Killer" (we'll get to that shortly) is responsible for the deaths of at least eight women, though some claim that the real number could be as high as 130. His first known victim was only 8 years old when he kidnapped, raped and attempted to murder her. He fled the scene of the crime and evaded capture for three years, eventually being added to the FBI's 'Ten Most Wanted' list. He was captured in 1974 but only served 34 months, allowing him to continue committing his despicable acts for another five years. During this time he took to photography, fooling people into believing he was a professional and persuading them into posing for pictures. Many of these being teenagers (both of age and underage), with a high number of sexually explicit images. Many photographs were found following his arrest and, though most of the subjects are unidentified, it is believed that many may be missing persons or cold case victims. Here are a few more facts about "The Dating Game Killer"...

He appeared on ABC's prime time show "The Dating Game"

I told you we'd get to it. Rodney Alcala received his moniker "The Dating Game Killer" due to the fact he appeared on the show, hosted by Jim Lange, in 1978. That's right, 1978, in the midst of his murderous crime spree. Not only did he make an appearance on the show, he won! For anybody unfamiliar with the show, this means he beat two other eligible bachelors to win a date with the bachelorette. Luckily for her, she sensed something was amiss and subsequently refused to go on the date after finding him 'creepy' when they met backstage, even going as for as saying she "started to feel ill."

Alcala acted as his own attorney

This fact doesn't seem all too interesting at first glance, many people have served as their own attorney (I'm looking at you, Bundy). However, Alcala had a slightly different approach. He interrogated himself, referring to himself in the third-person and speaking in a deep voice whilst questioning himself, and replying in first-person in his own voice when answering. If this isn't already strange enough, his opening statement was three weeks into the trial and began by questioning himself on his hair.

He was questioned over the Hillside Strangler murders

At the time, Alcala was working as a typesetter for the Los Angeles Times who were publishing articles about the Hillside Strangler who was terrorising the area. The task force assigned to the case decided to question all known sex offenders in the region, and as Alcala was a registered child rapist following the attempted murder of his first victim, he was on their radar. Though after a brief interview at his mothers home he was cleared of any involvement in the Hillside Strangler case.

Richard Chase

Murderers very often start out by killing and torturing animals as kids.

- Robert Ressler

Serial Killer Profile

Name: ———————————————— Richard Chase

Nickname: ——————— The Vampire of Sacramento

DOB: ———————————————— 05/23/50

Country: ———————————————— USA

Convicted murders: ——————————— 6

Estimated murders: ——————————— 6

Killing spree: ———————————— '77-'78

Caught: ————————————— 01/27/78

Modus operandi: ——————— Shooting

Victim profile: ————————— Varied

Sentence: ————————————— Death

Present: ——————— Deceased - Suicide

Richard Chase

The Vampire of Sacramento

The case of Richard Chase, also known as the "Vampire of Sacramento" was a very strange one. From a young age, Chase was a troubled individual, from wetting the bed to arson, to cruelty to animals, he ticked off all three boxes of the Macdonald triad. He was also a hypochondriac, claiming his heart would sometimes simply stop beating or that his arteries had been stolen. Of course, these delusions were only catalysed by the chronic drug use and alcohol consumption. He was involuntarily institutionalised for three years before being released in 1976. The following year he began his killing spree which, though only lasting two months, claimed the lives of six people. Here are some strange facts about the "Vampire of Sacramento"...

He drank the blood of his victims

The name kind of gives this one away. Along with the "Vampire of Sacramento" he was also known as the "Dracula Killer." His fixation with drinking blood began (or was first discovered) whilst institutionalised. He began catching birds through a window and proceeded to snap their necks and drink their blood, this led to the staff referring to him as "Dracula." The obsession with blood followed him out of the institute when the year after he was released he was found smeared in cows blood, along with a bucket full of it in his truck. Then, during his killing spree, he would drink his victim's blood, as well as engaging in cannibalism.

He would make blood smoothies

On occasion Chase would capture small animals, such as rats, and disembowel the creatures, eating them raw. He would also put the insides of the animals in a blender with coca cola in order to make the most disgusting smoothie imaginable. The concoction was allegedly a remedy to stop his heart from shrinking.

He injected the blood of animals

Due to his hypochondria, he sought to cure his non-existent illnesses. Though going to a doctor would usually be the first port of call, we're talking about a man who drinks animal guts milkshakes here. So to cure the various imaginary ailments he took to injecting the blood of animals. This was in fact what led to his institutionalisation when he contracted blood poisoning after injecting himself with the blood of a rabbit.

He would only enter unlocked houses

True to his vampire nature, Chase could not enter a home he had not been invited into. Only in Chase's case, an invitation simply meant an unlocked door. After his arrest, Chase told police that locked doors were a sign that he was not welcome, but an unlocked door was an all entry pass. As his only motivation for murder was bloodlust, this became the only contributing factor to how he chose his victims, trying door handles until he found an open door.

Dennis Rader

> *Waiting in the dark, waiting, waiting...*
>
> - Dennis Rader

Serial Killer Profile

Name: ———————————— Dennis Lynn Rader

Nickname: ———————————— BTK Killer

DOB: ———————————— 03/09/45

Country: ———————————— USA

Convicted murders: ———————————— 10

Estimated murders: ———————————— 10

Killing spree: ———————————— '74-'91

Caught: ———————————— 02/25/05

Modus operandi: ———————————— Asphyxiation

Victim profile: ———————— Female (usually older)

Sentence: ———————————— Life

Present: ———— El Dorado Correctional Facility

Dennis Rader

The BTK Killer

Dennis Rader was many things. A family man, a husband, a father, a heartless serial killer, you know, the usual. Rader does differ from many serial killers in a few ways, such as his communication with the police. Though it isn't unheard of for killers to taunt police, it is quite rare. The other difference is the sheer length of his "cool off" periods, along with the meticulous planning and arrangement that went into each crime. He plagued the state of Kansas between 1974 and 1991, though he did not get apprehended until 2005. One would be forgiven for thinking he had stopped in 1991, but this was just an extensive cool off period, and he was planning to kill again had he not been arrested. Rader claimed 10 victims during the span of his crimes, with no qualms as to whether they were men, women or children. Giving that he had children himself and was, for all intents and purposes, a good father shows how far detached from empathy and how void of emotion the man really was. Here are a few more facts about the "Bind, Torture, Kill" killer...

He was an alarm installation engineer

Not a very intriguing fact until you realise that this role helped him bypass the security of many of the homes he broke in to. Also, many of the customers were having alarms installed was to keep intruders out of their home following the reports of a killer on the loose. Ironically, in attempting to protect themselves they were welcoming that very killer into their homes.

He was really, really dumb

Though he was pursuing a degree in criminal justice, he was certainly not the sharpest tool in the shed. In 1977 he called the police to report a homicide, only his pronunciation was "h-O-micide", which police initially believed was a clue. Unfortunately not, it was just that he wasn't very intelligent which was subsequently proven in his written correspondence to police, as his letters were filled with spelling mistakes and grammatical errors. It is utterly amazing that a man who considers "I'm sorry this happen to society" to be a properly worded sentence was able to get away with murder for over 30 years.

He was dumb enough to trust the police not to lie to him

Remember how I said he was dumb? Even though he had gotten away with the murders of ten people for 14 years, his own ego got him caught. He heard of a lawyer who was writing a book about his case and refused to let him hog the limelight. So he began corresponding with police again. Growing weary of writing letters with pen and paper he asked police if he could send the writings via floppy disk, and if they could be traced this way. Of course, the police said they couldn't trace a floppy disk. Of course, the police **could** trace a floppy disk. When arrested Rader was more shocked at the fact police had lied to him than anything else.

Rader was a faithful husband

Say what you will about the monster, he was a gentleman. You see, in most of the incidents, Rader's semen was found at the scene, but never where you would expect it. On a cloth, on the floor, on a leg, this was due to the fact that radar would masturbate over the dead bodies of his victims, rather than rape them. It is alleged that he did not rape the victims due to his marriage vows and in order to stay faithful to his wife. Who said chivalry is dead?

Rader liked to take selfies

We aren't talking your run-of-the-mill Instagram-style selfie here. Rader enjoyed adorning female clothing, tying himself up in different scenarios, and taking photographs to later pleasure himself to. Photographs included:

- Rader wearing a blonde wig and a mask, tied to a chair with duct tape across his mouth
- Rader buried up to his chest in mud, wearing a white mask with tape over his mouth
- Rader wearing a dress whilst suspended from a tree with rope
- Rader wearing a red bra and mask with his hands tied behind his back, laid out on the floor

There are many more, as Rader used to be so overcome with desires for bondage he would try and recreate his own crime scenes for photographs, playing the victim himself.

Pedro Lopez

You asked me if I felt anything while asphyxiating certain persons? Well, no. Is it strange, no?

- Pedro Lopez

Serial Killer Profile

Name: ———————————— Pedro Alonso López

Nickname: ———————— The Monster of the Andes

DOB: ————————————————————— 10/08/48

Country: ———————————————————— Columbia

Convicted murders: ————————————— 110

Estimated murders: ————————————— 300

Killing spree: ——————————————————— '69-'80

Caught: ——————————————————— 03/09/80

Modus operandi: ————— Stabbing/strangulation

Victim profile: ———————————————— Young girls

Sentence: ————————————— 16 years (served 14)

Present: ————————————————————— Unknown

Pedro Lopez

The Monster of the Andes

'The Monster of the Andes' was a very fitting title for Pedro Lopez. His body count is one of the highest in history. Lopez whole life was tragic. He was born in Colombia in the 40's where his father was shot dead before he was born and his mother was a sex worker. He was kicked out of his home at the age of 8 for molesting his sister. He was abused several times as a young boy, including getting raped in an empty house he had sought refuge in. By the time of his arrest, he had killed at least 110 people, primarily young girls, though by his own claims the actual body count is over 300. Here are some more unbelievable facts about the man...

He committed his first murder in prison

Lopez was serving a sentence for car theft when he was set upon by a gang of inmates. The men beat him badly and gang raped him. His revenge was something you may expect from a Quentin Tarantino movie. He made a knife in his cell and visited the men who had attacked him one by one until he had killed them all.

He was almost stopped

A local indigenous tribe thwarted an attempt by Lopez to kidnap a 9-year-old girl. Upon capturing him they sought to execute him by burying him alive. They were preparing to do so when a Christian missionary intercepted and they agreed to hand him over to the local authority. Unfortunately, once he was in police custody he was released and continued his murderous rampage.

Nobody believed him

He was arrested again several years later trying to kidnap another girl. When he would not cooperate an undercover operation was put in place, during which he confessed to over 300 murders. However, with such a high number the authorities were sceptical, until a mass grave was uncovered by a flash flood.

Random Fact

Following a complaint about a "foul stench" and smoke billowing from the chimney, firefighters were called out to Marcel Petiot's house by neighbours. They found that in the fire were human remains. Marcel Petiot went into hiding under the alias "Henri Valeri" eventually working for the French Forces of the Interior. After evidence emerged that the killer may still be in Paris a team was put together to find and capture him. Henri Valeri (A.K.A Marcel Petiot himself) was on the team tasked with the search.

Nobody knows where he is

One of the most notorious serial killers in the world, with a body count in the triple digits who was officially declared insane, you would think his whereabouts would be watched very closely. After being arrested in 1981 he was sentenced to the maximum sentence available in Ecuador at the time. 16 years. The abysmal sentencing meant that in 1994 he was eligible to be released, which he was, on $50 bail. Lopez was then transferred to a mental institution in Columbia. Only four years later he was declared sane and released. Since then, information on his whereabouts has been minimal, though some sources say he is still in prison, others say he simply disappeared and is living his life a free man. If the latter is true then it may be one of the greatest miscarriages of justice in history, along with one of the most dangerous decisions ever made by a judicial system.

Random Fact

Chris Clarke was apprehensive about his mother's new boyfriend, Ray Constantine. But after Ray got Chris a job and they began working together they became good friends. One day whilst Chris was 35ft up a ladder at work painting, it began to slide. Ray came rushing from the yard to a third storey window and willed Chris to shunt the heavy ladder back into place. Chris was frozen with fear but thanks to the encouragement of Ray Chris snapped out of it and forced the ladder back into place, which Ray swiftly tied up to enable Chris to get down. Chris would not find out until his mother and Ray parted ways, that Ray's real name was Stephen Morin, and he was responsible for the murders of at least 4 people.

Ted Bundy

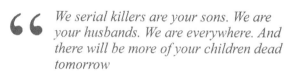

We serial killers are your sons. We are your husbands. We are everywhere. And there will be more of your children dead tomorrow

- Ted Bundy

Serial Killer Profile

Name: ———————————— Theodore Robert Cowell

Nickname: ———————————————— Ted Bundy

DOB: ——————————————————— 11/24/46

Country: ————————————————————— USA

Convicted murders: ———————————— 30

Estimated murders: ——————————— 100+

Killing spree: ——————————————— '74-'78

Caught: ———————————————— 02/15/78

Modus operandi: —— Abduction, rape and murder

Victim profile: ——— Young, brunette women

Sentence: ——————————————— Death

Present: ————————— Deceased - Electric Chair

Ted Bundy

The Poster Boy

Ted Bundy was one of the most cold-hearted serial killers America has ever seen. He was convicted of murdering 30 victims, though the actual body count could be much higher than this. His youngest victim was just a 12-year-old girl, and though he eventually admitted to his crimes (after a lengthy process of trying to convince the world, and possibly himself, that he was innocent) he showed little, if any, remorse. So it would come as a shock to many people that, during certain points of his life, he actually managed to display some human emotions. Here are a few things you may not know about the man...

He once saved a boy from drowning

Bundy was in Green Lake, Seattle, when he saw a young boy wandering away from his parents. The boy got too close to the lake and fell in, which is when Bundy jumped into the lake after him and stopped the poor boy from drowning. I don't think we'll ever quite know why he wanted to save a life when he so badly wanted to take them also.

He offered his help in catching the Green River Killer

Bundy wrote to Keppel and Reichart, who were in charge of the Green River Killer case, offering to give them a serial killers perspective on the case. He did give them some useful information, such as telling them that the killer would most likely return to the bodies to engage in necrophilia, and their best chance of finding the killer would be to find a fresh body and lay in wait. Though the information turned out to be spot on, corpses are not all too easy to come by and the Green River Killer would not be caught for a further 17 years.

He worked at a suicide prevention hotline

One of the most infamous killers on the planet once spent his days trying to keep people alive. The irony is palpable. You would be forgiven for thinking he may have just done this for a paycheck, however, former colleagues of his have noted he was very good at his job. One of his former colleagues just so happens to be the great true crime author, Ann Rule. She has been quoted on one occasion as saying "Ted Bundy took lives, but he also saved lives".

If you haven't read Ann Rules #1 New York Times Best Seller **"The Stranger Beside Me"**, which details her time at the crisis hotline with Bundy, then this author would highly recommend it.

He escaped custody

Bundy was arrested for the first time after being pulled over by a state trooper who found a crowbar, ski mask, rope, wire, an icepick and handcuffs in his car, along with the passenger seat missing. He was then picked out of a line-up by a victim who had managed to escape him after being kidnapped. Whilst he was serving time for the kidnapping, police were linking him to other crimes, including several murders. As he decided to represent himself in court, he was excused from wearing handcuffs or shackles and allowed to visit the courthouse library to research for his case. Once in the library he found an open window behind a bookcase and proceeded to jump from the second floor. Though he sprained his ankle upon landing, he still managed to disappear toward Aspen Mountain. Six days later he was caught driving a stolen car swerving across lanes (due to the pain of his ankle and sleep deprivation) and taken back to jail.

He escaped custody... again

You read that right. Not only did he manage to escape once, in regular Harry Houdini style, he managed to get out a second time. Though there was very little evidence against him in the case, he still chose to have a hacksaw smuggled in, along with $500 cash over various visits. After finding a small hole behind a light fitting he began to saw what would become an exit around a square foot. He had to lose over 30 pounds to be able to squeeze through, which is exactly what he did. That night he walked out of the front door. This time he wouldn't be caught for several weeks, committing many atrocious acts within that time, one of which became one of the strongest cases against him, and helped secure him the death penalty.

He stopped a thief who snatched a lady's purse

After witnessing a robber make off with a woman's purse in a mall he leapt into pursuit, chasing and eventually catching the felon. For this, he was commended by the police department and even received a letter of gratitude from the governor of Washington.

He may have attempted to kidnap Blondie's Debbie Harry

Firstly, the details of this one don't quite add up. However, there are some striking similarities between Debbie's horrifying ordeal and the way Bundy operated. In the early 70's before 'Blondie' fame, in the early hours of the morning, Debbie was attempting to get a cab when a small white car pulled up beside her. The man offered her a ride, and as it was only a couple of blocks away she accepted. Once in the car she reached for the window crank and realised there wasn't one. Upon looking at the door she then realised there was no handle either, in fact, the whole car seemed to be stripped out. Not fancying being trapped in a car with a strange man and no way out, she put her hand through the small crack in the window and opened the door from the outside. When the man saw her doing this he seemed to speed up, and Debbie flew out of the car, landing in the middle of the road. Debbie believes the man was Bundy, though it has been determined that Bundy would not have been in New York during this period of time.

Random Fact

Arthur Shawcross was troublesome from a young age. After years of petty crime, burglary, theft and more, Shawcross was sentenced to five years in prison for two counts of arson. During his time in prison, a racially charged riot broke out. A correctional officer was cornered and being beaten mercilessly by several inmates when Shawcross stepped in and pulled the officer out of harm's way, quite possibly saving his life in the process. For this act Shawcross was paroled early, serving only 22 months of his five-year sentence. A kind act for a man who went on to kill 14 people, including an 8-year-old girl and 11-year-old boy.

H. H. Holmes

I was born with the devil in me. I could not help the fact that I was a murderer, no more than the poet can help the inspiration to sing...I was born with the evil one standing as my sponsor beside the bed where I was ushered into the world, and he has been with me since.

- H. H. Holmes

Serial Killer Profile

Name: ———————— Herman Webster Mudgett

Nickname: ———————— Henry Howard Holmes

DOB: ———————————— 05/16/1861

Country: ————————————— USA

Convicted murders: ——————— Approx. 9

Estimated murders: ——————— 27-200+

Killing spree: ———————— 1891-1894

Caught: ———————————— 11/17/1894

Modus operandi: ——————— Varied

Victim profile: ——————— Varied

Sentence: ——————————— Death

Present: ——————— Deceased - Hanging

H. H. Holmes

America's First Serial Killer

America's first serial killer. This is what H.H. Holmes is widely known as, as well as "The American Ripper." The latter is fitting for the man, as many suspect him of being Jack the Ripper himself. Though the evidence is largely circumstantial there is some weight to the theory. There were some American-isms in letters from Jack, Holmes was a doctor as Jack was believed to be, the forensic sketch of Jack bears a striking similarity to Holmes, and Holmes business records seemed to disappear during the times of the Whitechapel murders. There was also evidence of a passenger named "H. Holmes" travelling back to the states from England following the murders. Here are a few more facts about Holmes...

He built a "Murder Castle"

The World's Fair Hotel was a tourist trap, in the literal sense. Once you were in it was almost impossible to get out. There were over 50 doorways that opened up into brick walls, staircases that led to nothing, windowless rooms, gas chambers, a 'hanging' room, trap doors and more.

He would strip the flesh of the dead

Once he had trapped his victims he would kill them using a variety of methods, but the end game was usually the same. They would be skinned and dissected, eventually, all that would be left was their skeleton, which he would sell to medical schools. The financial gain seemed to be one of his biggest motives as he would usually claim the life insurance of the victims.

He was a player

Holmes wasn't just a murderer and fraudster, he was also a bigamist. In 1878 at 16 he married Clara Lovering. Six years later, after growing tired of his violence, Clara moved back to New Hampshire with their son, but without Holmes. In 1886 he married Myrta Belknap and they had a daughter, all the while Holmes was still married to Lovering. Then in 1894, whilst still married to both Lovering and Belknap, Holmes married a third woman named Georgiana Yoke.

Richard Ramirez

*We are all evil in some form or another,
are we not?*

- Richard Ramirez

Serial Killer Profile

Name: ———————————— Richard Ramirez

Nickname: ———————— The Night Stalker

DOB: ———————————————— 02/29/1960

Country: ———————————————— USA

Convicted murders: ———————— 14

Estimated murders: ———————— 14

Killing spree: ———————— '84-'85

Caught: ———————————— 08/31/85

Modus operandi: ———————— Stabbing/shooting

Victim profile: ———————— Varied

Sentence: ———————————— Death

Present: ———————— Deceased - Health issues

Richard Ramirez

The Night Stalker

Ramirez, A.K.A "The Night Stalker" was not just cold-hearted, he lacked empathy completely. As he was a satanist, not only did he commit the crimes, but he thrived off of the notion that this would appease the devil himself. However, his crimes were not merely for sacrificial purposes, they were also financially motivated in order to fund his $1000+ a week drug habit. In less than 18 months Ramirez would take the lives of 14 innocent people, including a 9-year-old girl and an 83-year-old woman. He would eventually be caught and receive the death penalty, but justice was never truly served, as he died due to complications with B-cell lymphoma before he ever made it near the gas chamber. At the time of his death he still had many appeals pending. Here are some of the stranger facts about "The Night Stalker"...

Ramirez threatened to kill the prosecution

Ramirez never showed any remorse for his crimes, quite the opposite in fact. Not only did he smile and laugh during his trial, he even sought to continue his reign of terror by threatening to kill the prosecution. As he was already in custody this could quite easily have been regarded as an empty threat, however, it seemed to carry a lot more weight when one of the jurors was found murdered in her home. You would be forgiven for thinking that the two things were related, but it turned out to be the juror's boyfriend who committed the terrible act and unrelated to the trial itself.

He spent time in prison with Todd Bridges

That's right, Willis from 'Diff'rent Strokes' served time in prison with The Night Stalker. Bridges was allegedly involved in the shooting of a drug dealer in LA and sent down for attempted murder, though he has since been acquitted. Bridges states that Ramirez used to shake the bars to his cell and say "I'm going to come in and get you" before displaying the pentagram tattoo on his palm. Though Bridges says the day Ramirez found out he was getting the gas chamber he was a different man, quiet, maybe even scared... hopefully.

Random Fact

Charles Manson. You've probably heard of him before, maybe read about him in a book about serial killers, or seen his picture above a list of the "Ten Worst Serial Killers." He's often cited to be one of the worst serial killers to walk the Earth. The only problem with this claim is that he isn't a serial killer. Actually, he isn't a killer at all, in the literal sense. Manson never killed anybody with his own hands, rather he persuaded his naive and unstable followers to kill for him.

Jeffrey Dahmer

It's hard for me to believe that a human being could have done what I've done, but I know that I did it.

\- Jeffrey Dahmer

Serial Killer Profile

Name: ———————————— Jeffrey Dahmer

Nickname: ————— The Milwaukee Cannibal

DOB: ———————————— 05/21/60

Country: ———————————— USA

Convicted murders: ————————— 17

Estimated murders: ————————— 17

Killing spree: ————————— '78-'91

Caught: ———————————— 07/22/91

Modus operandi: ————— Drug/strangulation

Victim profile: ————— Young black males

Sentence: ———————————— Life

Present: ————— Deceased - Homicide

Jeffrey Dahmer

The Milwaukee Cannibal

The story of Jeffrey Dahmer tells like something from a Rob Zombie movie. Unfortunately, this story is all too true. Between 1978 and 1991 Dahmer raped, murdered and dismembered 17 young men and boys. He killed out of loneliness, in order to keep his company he would usually drug the victim and asphyxiate them until death. He would then keep the body laying around his apartment for days, placing the body in several positions and photographing it. He also engaged in necrophilia, would chop the body into pieces, fillet the bones, engage in cannibalism, and keep souvenirs such as skulls and genitals. For a more in-depth look into Dahmer's life and actions check out my book "The Ones Who Got Away." For now, let's take a look at some of the strange facts about Dahmer...

He tried to create a living zombie

The most heartbreaking part of this story is that the victim was just a 14-year-old boy. After drugging Konerak Sinthasomphone, Dahmer drilled a hole in the boys head and injected hydrochloric acid into his brain. He believed this would make Sinthasomphone enter a zombie-like state. When Sinthasomphone awoke he was seemingly incapacitated.

He nearly got caught

After he had injected Sinthasomphone with acid, he felt confident enough that the boy was now completely incapacitated to leave him in his apartment while he headed to a local bar. However, Sinthasomphone escaped and flagged down a couple of women in search of help. As the young boy was naked and bleeding the girls called the police, but Dahmer turned up first. The pair of women refused to let Sinthasomphone leave with Dahmer and awaited the arrival of the police. But somehow the sociopath managed to fool the police into believing that the 14-year-old was his 19-year-old boyfriend and that he was just drunk and had caused an argument. Sinthasomphone's life ended at the hands of Dahmer that night.

The man who helped catch Dahmer was arrested for homicide himself

Tracy Edwards was Dahmer's last intended victim. After trying to handcuff Edwards and failing Dahmer explained that he was going to kill him that evening. However, Dahmer had a slight lapse in concentration during one of Edwards bathroom trips, and when Edwards saw his chance he took it. He punched Dahmer in the face and escaped through the unlocked door. Edwards then took police back to the apartment where Dahmer was arrested. However, 20 years later Edwards himself was charged with the murder of a homeless man by throwing him off a bridge. Edwards received 18 months in prison on a lesser charge of aiding a felon.

Dahmer didn't wear glasses during his trial

Most pictures you see of Dahmer include his signature glasses. However, those who have watched the trial itself will notice he did not have his glasses on. In his own words, this was because he "felt uncomfortable looking anybody in the face" and because he "didn't want to see anyone's face clearly" this helped him disassociate himself from what was happening.

He liked to brag about his crimes

Whilst in prison he liked to talk. He also liked to fashion his meals to look like human limbs and would smother them with ketchup to simulate blood. Acting in such a way would eventually lead to his death. He was left alone to clean bathrooms with Jesse Anderson and Christopher Scarver. Scarver was a prisoner who despised Dahmer and all he had done. He confronted Dahmer with a newspaper detailing his crimes before cracking his skull with a metal bar twice, killing him. He also attacked Jesse Anderson who succumb to his injuries two days later.

He planned to build a shrine from the body parts of his victims

There was even a hand-drawn plan detailing his shrine, which included painted skulls, painted skeletons, a black and white carpet, and a black plush chair. Amongst the plans for the shrine here are some other things police found in Dahmer's apartment:

- A severed head in a cardboard box
- Two severed hands
- Two human hearts
- Male genitals & mummified genitals
- A bag full of flesh and organs
- A bag containing a human muscle
- Several human skulls
- A complete human skeleton
- Three human torsos inside a blue plastic drum

Edmund Kemper

> *I stabbed her, but she didn't fall dead.*
> *They're supposed to go 'oh!' and fall*
> *dead, thats how it goes in movies, right?*
> *It didn't go that way. When you stab*
> *somebody, they leak to death.*

- Edmund Kemper

Serial Killer Profile

Name: ———————————— Edmund Kemper

Nickname: ——————————— The Co-ed Killer

DOB: ——————————————— 12/18/48

Country: ——————————————— USA

Convicted murders: ————————— 10

Estimated murders: ————————— 10

Killing spree: ————————— '64-'73

Caught: ——————————— 04/24/73

Modus operandi: —— Post-mortem decapitation

Victim profile: —————— Young co-ed women

Sentence: ———————————— Life

Present: ———— California Medical Facility

Edmund Kemper

The Co-ed Killer

Ed Kemper, A.K.A "The Co-ed Killer" was once thought to be a gentle giant. He was a very polite, well-spoken young man, which helped him lure young college students into his car, and standing at 6 foot 9 inch there was very little chance of them escaping once he had made his mind up to kill them. Ed's murderous tendencies began when he killed both his grandparents at the age of 15, though he spent only six years in a criminally insane unit before being released upon the world again. He began killing college students as a way to get back at his mother for her poor treatment of him. Of course, his mother was none-the-wiser and so this had little effect on their relationship, at which point he knew that this could only stop once he killed his mother herself. Here are some facts about "The Co-ed Killer"...

After killing his own mother he sodomized her decapitated head

You read that right. Not only did he bludgeon his mother to death with a claw hammer and slit her throat, he then proceeded to engage in sexual activity with the severed head, as well as the corpse. Stating his mother used to complain she hadn't had sex in seven years because of her murderous son, and so he "humiliated her corpse."

He once 'saved the life' of two girls

'Saving their lives' was his own take on it. You see, he originally picked them up to see if he could control the urge to kill them. Let that sink in. He picked up two young ladies, very similar in appearance to the two young ladies he had killed at the beginning of his second wave of killings. He offered them a lift to their campus and they requested he go a certain route. He knew the route lead right past the quiet location of one of his previous killings, and so he refused to go that route. His refusal scared the girls, who then began to think that he was taking them somewhere else. It's all a bit backwards, because had he gone the way they asked, they would not have been scared, but they would have been dead. And thus, he saved their lives... or at least he didn't kill them.

He has narrated many audio books for the blind

He was the head of the whole program in the late 1970's, recording more than 5000 hours worth of audio, which equates to over 4 million feet of tape. Some of the titles include:

- Flowers in the Attic
- Petals on the Wind
- The Rosary Murders
- Sphinx
- Star Wars & more

He performed behaviour modification experiments on serial killer Herbert Mullin

Ed Kemper and Herbert Mullin terrorised the Santa Cruz area simultaneously. They were also both apprehended less than two months apart. They were then housed in adjoining cells. And they really took a disliking to each other. Mullin, standing at 5 foot 7 inch, wouldn't be so foolish as to get physical with the enormous Kemper, and instead took to singing loudly and annoying people whilst they tried to watch television. Kemper began to throw water on him through the cell doors each time he did this, but he would give him peanuts when he had been good. Soon enough Mullin was asking for permission before singing.

Random Fact

Full-time pig farmer and part-time serial killer Robert Pickton used to pick up prostitutes in Vancouver and take them back to his farm on the promise of money and drugs. He would then kill them and feed them to his pigs. Pickton was caught by chance after a truck driver spotted some illegal guns on his property. Police raided the farm for the weapons and came across a whole host of items belonging to missing women. His only regret, in his own words, was "I wanted one more to make the big five-0." Though this exchange was recorded on camera by an undercover officer, he later wrote a book protesting his innocence and claiming the Canadian police simply needed a fall guy. The book, published on Amazon, was quickly pulled from the shelves after it caused outrage amongst the victim's families.

John Wayne Gacy

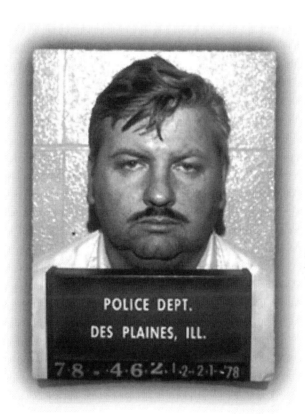

" *The dead won't bother you, it's the living you have to worry about.*

- John Wayne Gacy **"**

Serial Killer Profile

Name: ———————————— John Wayne Gacy

Nickname: ———————————— The Killer Clown

DOB: ———————————— 03/17/42

Country: ———————————— USA

Convicted murders: ———————————— 33

Estimated murders: ———————————— 33+

Killing spree: ———————————— '72-'78

Caught: ———————————— 12/21/78

Modus operandi: ———— Rape/strangulation

Victim profile: ———— Young men and boys

Sentence: ———————————— Death

Present: ———— Deceased - Lethal injection

John Wayne Gacy
The Killer Clown

John Wayne Gacy was a family man, successful business owner, politician, and serial killer. He was convicted of the murders of 33 young men and boys, all of which were committed in his own home and the majority buried in his crawl space. On the outside he was a stand-up guy, owning a construction contracting business as well as being a community volunteer, serving on the director's board of Jaycees, being involved in the democratic party, and even meeting then First Lady Rosalyn Carter. However, the man he portrayed on the outside was a far throw away from the man he was on the inside. After years of mental and physical abuse at the hands of his father Gacy had learned to only show the parts of him that he believed the world wanted to see, even hiding his homosexuality to the point where he married and had children. Thanks to the practice he had in trying to please his father all those years he had become good at hiding his true self by the time he started killing. Here are a few more twisted facts about Gacy...

His first murder was 'self-defence'... well, not really

Don't get me wrong, Gacy was not a nice man who 'accidentally' hurt people. Even before his first murder, he had a history of sexually abusing male teenagers, including one incident for which he was sentenced to 10 years in prison, though he was released after 18 months. In 1972 Gacy picked up a 16-year-old boy who he brought back to his house to spend the night. He woke up in the morning to the boy stood in his doorway with a knife. A struggle ensued and, even though Gacy could quite easily have overpowered the young boy and restrained him, he instead twisted the boy's wrist in order to get the knife and stabbed him multiple times in the chest. Gacy walked from his bedroom to find the boy had just been preparing breakfast.

He was the real-life Pennywise

That's right, he was a killer clown. Of course, this is where he gained his nickname "The Killer Clown" as he was part of the "Jolly Joker Club" whose members would dress as clowns to volunteer at fundraisers and hospitals. Gacy's clown persona was named "Pogo the Clown" and he would sometimes turn up to his local bar for a drink dressed in full clown attire.

He used power, trust, and deceit to subdue his victims

As he owned a construction company he employed many young men and teenagers as labourers. He would invite some of the boys to his house where he would get them drunk and high and then offer to show them a trick. "The Handcuff Trick" was where Gacy would show the victim how to get free should they ever be in a situation where they are handcuffed. The boys, of course, trusted their boss and thought this was just a magic trick (after all, he was a clown) and agreed to be handcuffed. Once the handcuffs were on Gacy would reveal the trick to getting free... "The trick is, you have to have the key." He would then kill the victim with "The Rope Trick."

He became an artist in prison

Of course, most of his paintings were of clowns, what else was it going to be? He would become one of the most famous incarcerated painters and his paintings are still selling for thousands, though many were bought by the victims family's and burned.

His last meal was KFC

Before he started his construction business, Gacy ran multiple KFC restaurants. He would bring KFC chicken to his Jaycee meetings and ask his Jaycees colleagues to call him "The Colonel." Therefore, it was fitting that for his last meal he asked for a bucket of KFC, french fries, fried shrimp and strawberries.

Random Fact

The Axeman of New Orleans was responsible for at least 6 murders and 12 attacks over the course of a year in the early 20th century. During the height of his crime spree, he wrote a letter which was published in the press stating that he would kill again at exactly 12:15 AM that coming Tuesday. He did, however, leave the people a choice. He stated that he loved jazz music and would spare the lives of anybody who had a jazz band playing. When Tuesday night came, the whole city of New Orleans was bustling and you could not escape the sound of jazz music. In the dance halls and clubs, even in many private residences jazz bands were in full swing. That night there were no murders.

Random Facts

The Fall Guy

David Allen Jones was a convicted serial killer, having been found guilty of the murder of three women. This, however, was a huge miscarriage of justice, considering Jones hadn't killed anybody, he had the mental capacity of an 8-year-old, was classified as mentally retarded, there was no evidence to link him to the crimes, and the DNA found at the crime scenes did not match his. Jones was by no means a saint, but all the police had was a confession that had been coerced over the course of two days and a previous arrest from when Jones was found with a prostitute at the school he worked at many years earlier. Fast-forward 11 years and the DNA evidence linked the crimes to serial killer Chester Turner. After spending 11 years in prison for crimes he did not commit Jones was exonerated.

The Worst Serial Killer in History

Luis Garavito has gained several labels for his crimes, such as 'The Beast' and 'The Worst Serial Killer in History'. His crimes? Killing a minimum of 138 young boys. 138 is the number of confirmed victims, but he himself claims to have killed more than 400. For the heinous acts, he was sentenced to a total of 1853 years in prison. Sounds good, except that Colombian law limits imprisonment to 40 years, and as he helped the authorities during the investigation his sentence was reduced to merely 22 years. That is less than 2 months per (convicted) murder. Fortunately, there are conflicting laws that look to keep Garavito behind bars for at least 60 years.

Checkmate

Alexander Pichushkin was one of the worst serial killers Russia has ever seen. He gained the nickname "The Chessboard Killer" due to the fact he boasted he wanted to kill 64 people, one for every square on the chessboard. Unfortunately for him, he was stopped just short at 63, or at least these are his claims, as he was only convicted of 48. He was caught after killing a woman who had left a note at her home saying she had gone for a walk with him. Though he was aware of the note and its possible implications, he said he could not stop himself from killing her.

The Murdermobile

The Toy Box Killer, real name David Parker Ray, gained his infamous nickname from his trailer, which he called his 'toy-box'. The trailer was kitted out with over $100,000 worth of rape and torture gear, including sex toys, syringes, an operating table, whips and chains, surgical equipment and more. He would kidnap women and bring them back to the trailer, and with the help of his family and friends torture them for days before killing them.

The Non-performer

The Rostov Ripper was responsible for the killings of at least 52 women and children. His first murder began as a rape, however, when he could not get an erection he killed the young girl. He ejaculated whilst stabbing the victim, and from this incident, he was no longer able to achieve orgasm unless it was during killing another human being.

To Catch a Killer

The Yorkshire Ripper, Peter Sutcliffe, got away with his crimes for far too long considering how flippant he was with his actions. Not only were their many survivors who were able to give evidence and descriptions, but he was on the police radar from the beginning. Sutcliffe was interviewed a total of nine times by police. Let me repeat that, nine whole times. Due to a horrendous breakdown in communication, the interviewing officers were almost never aware of previous interviews, allowing Sutcliffe to continue killing for much too long.

The Hunter

One serial killer went to extreme lengths to satisfy his twisted need to kill Robert Hansen would pick up young women or sex workers in Alaska, and after raping them he would fly them out into the middle of the Alaskan wilderness, then set them free. But they weren't free, Hansen would follow their tracks, hunt them down, and kill them like animals. Until a young lady managed to escape his clutches and expose his sick ways.

The Non-believers

Several months before serial killer Robert Berdella's arrest and conviction he was drinking at a bar. He drank too much and was over the legal driving limit when some fellow patrons offered him a ride home. Along the way, Berdella was drunkenly rambling when he started making shocking claims. Berdella was sprouting stories of kidnapping and torturing young men. Unfortunately, these claims were dismissed as the ramblings of a drunk man and were not reported at the time.

Murder Burger

Joe Metheny's killing spree was sparked by revenge. After his drug-addicted wife left him and took their son with her he flew off the handle and killed two homeless men his wife used to do drugs with. He was sent to jail but acquitted at trial due to lack of evidence. Once out he found he had a lust for murder. As he had gotten away with the first murder due to the fact there was no body, he knew he needed to get rid of the corpses of his victims permanently. He began mixing up the human flesh with beef and pork and opened up a barbecue stand, selling the 'evidence' of his crimes for human consumption.

Quick Fire Round

- Leonarda Cianciulli made soap from the fat of her victims
- Ashton Kutcher's former girlfriend was the victim of a serial killer
- 29 needles were found inserted in the serial killer and masochist Albert Fish's pelvis on arrest
- Whilst serving as town mayor, Dr Marcel Petiot was an active serial killer
- Vlado Taneski, a crime reporter, was also a serial killer. He was caught after writing articles about his crimes which included details never made public
- By some estimates, there are approximately 2000 active serial killers at-large in the US
- There was allegedly a serial killer in 16th century Germany who lived in a cave and killed 964 people
- In Canada, there is a 450mi long road called the "Highway of Tears". Since 1969 at least 19 (estimates of over 40) women have gone missing here, presumably murdered by one or more serial killers

Quotes

Quotes

There are very few people who will ever know what goes on in the mind of a serial killer. In fact, the only people who truly do are the serial killers themselves, and it is a rarity that they want to divulge all of the sick and twisted thoughts they conjure up.

The closest thing we can get to what is in their minds is what comes out of their mouths. Some serial killers are ashamed of what they have done, they show remorse and regret and hate to talk about their crimes. Some refuse to admit they ever even committed the crime, and despite an abundance of solid evidence, they will claim innocence until their last breath.

Then there are the few who relish the retelling of their crimes. The ones who are proud of their incomprehensible actions, and take pleasure from recounting each and every individual detail of their crimes and what is going on in their mind. They glorify themselves, they speak out for fame and want to be remembered for the heinous acts they have committed. Truly horrifying though it is, the ramblings of these monsters are as close as we will get to being inside the mind of a serial killer.

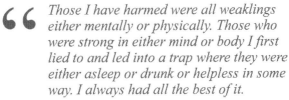

> *Those I have harmed were all weaklings either mentally or physically. Those who were strong in either mind or body I first lied to and led into a trap where they were either asleep or drunk or helpless in some way. I always had all the best of it.*

- Carl Panzram

> *In my lifetime I have murdered 21 human beings, I have committed thousands of burglaries, robberies, larcenies, arsons and, last but not least, I have committed sodomy on more than 1,000 male human beings. For all these things I am not in the least bit sorry.*

- Carl Panzram

> *I believe the only way to reform people is to kill them.*

- Carl Panzram

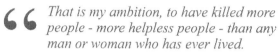

" *That is my ambition, to have killed more people - more helpless people - than any man or woman who has ever lived.* "

- Jane Toppan

" *I took the right leg of that woman's body, from the knee to the hip, took the fat off and ate it while she stared at the other girl. When I bit into it she just urinated right there.* "

- Arthur Shawcross

" *A clown can get away with murder.* "

- John Wayne Gacy

> *I always had the desire to inflict pain on others and to have others inflict pain on me. I always seemed to enjoy everything that hurt. The desire to inflict pain, that is all that is uppermost*

- Albert Fish

> *I like children, they are tasty.*

- Albert Fish

> *What a thrill that will be if I have to die in the electric chair. It will be the supreme thrill. The only one I haven't tried.*

- Albert Fish

> **To me, this world is nothing but evil, and my own evil just happened to come out 'cause of the circumstances of what I was doing.**
>
> - Aileen Wuornos

> **I robbed them, and I killed them as cold as ice, and I would do it again, and I know I would kill another person because I've hated humans for a long time.**
>
> - Aileen Wuornos

> **I am a serial killer. I would kill again.**
>
> - Aileen Wuornos

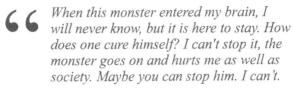

> *When this monster entered my brain, I will never know, but it is here to stay. How does one cure himself? I can't stop it, the monster goes on and hurts me as well as society. Maybe you can stop him. I can't.*

- Dennis Rader

> *I actually think I may be possessed with demons; I was dropped on my head as a kid.*

- Dennis rader

> *'It was this moment that victim was tied and bound.' He could live in that moment for years.*

- Sam Houston

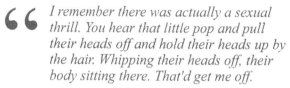

" *I remember there was actually a sexual thrill. You hear that little pop and pull their heads off and hold their heads up by the hair. Whipping their heads off, their body sitting there. That'd get me off.* "

- Edmund Kemper

" *I just wanted to see how it felt to shoot Grandma.* "

- Edmund Kemper

" *When I see a pretty girl walking down the street, I think two things: one part of me wants to take her home, be real nice and treat her right; the other part wonders what her head would look like on a stick.* "

- Edmund Kemper

You learn what you need to kill and take care of the details. It's like changing a tire. The first time you're careful. By the 30th time, you can't remember where you left the lug wrench.

- Ted Bundy

I'm the most cold-hearted son-of-a-bitch you'll ever meet.

- Ted Bundy

You feel the last bit of breath leaving their body. You're looking into their eyes. A person in that situation is God!

- Ted Bundy

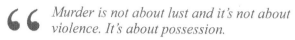

Murder is not about lust and it's not about violence. It's about possession.

- Ted Bundy

What's one less person on the face of the earth, anyway?

- Ted Bundy

There lots of other kids playing in streets around this country today who are going to be dead tomorrow, and the next day, and the next day and month, because other young people are reading the kinds of things and seeing the kinds of things that are available in the media today.

- Ted Bundy

" *I think most humans have within them the capacity to commit murder.*

- Richard Ramirez "

" *I've killed 20 people, man. I love all that blood.*

- Richard Ramirez "

" *Killing is killing whether done for duty, profit, or fun.*

- Richard Ramirez "

" *Big deal. Death comes with the territory. See you in Disneyland.*

- Richard Ramirez "

Yes, I do have remorse, but I'm not even sure myself whether it is as profound as it should be. I've always wondered myself why I don't feel more remorse.

- Jeffrey Dahmer

The killing was a means to an end. That's why I tried to create living zombies with uric acid and the drill, but it never worked. I just wanted to have the person under my complete control, not having to consider their wishes, being able to keep them there as long as I wanted.

- Jeffrey Dahmer

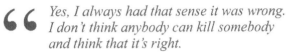

" *Yes, I always had that sense it was wrong. I don't think anybody can kill somebody and think that it's right.*

- Jeffrey Dahmer

"

" *I was completely swept along with my own compulsion. I don't know how else to put it. It didn't satisfy me completely, so maybe I was thinking, 'Maybe another one will. Maybe this one will.' And the numbers started growing and growing and just got out of control, as you can see.*

- Jeffrey Dahmer

"

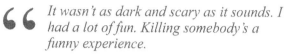

> *It wasn't as dark and scary as it sounds. I had a lot of fun. Killing somebody's a funny experience.*
>
> - Albert DeSalvo

> *The women I killed were filth-bastard prostitutes who were littering the streets. I was just cleaning up the place a bit.*
>
> - Peter Sutcliffe

> *After my head has been chopped off, will I still be able to hear, at least for a moment, the sound of my own blood gushing from my neck? That would be the best pleasure to end all pleasure.*
>
> - Peter Kurten

> *All of a sudden I realized that I had just done something that could never be undone. I realized that from that point on I could never be like normal people. I must have stood there in that state for 20 minutes. I have never felt an emptiness of self like I did right then and I will never forget that feeling. It was like I crossed over into a realm I could never come back from.*

- David Alan Gore

> *Sex is one of my downfalls. I get sex any way I can get it. If I have to force somebody to do it, I do. I rape them, I've done that. I've killed animals to have sex with them, and I've had sex while they're alive.*

- Henry Lee Lucas

" *I was literally singing to myself on my way home, after the killing. The tension, the desire to kill a woman had built up in such explosive proportions that when I finally pulled the trigger, all the pressure, all the tensions, all the hatred, had just vanished, dissipated, but only for a short time.*

\- David Berkowitz "

" *I don't believe in man, God nor Devil. I hate the whole damned human race, including myself. I preyed upon the weak, the harmless and the unsuspecting. This lesson I was taught by others: Might makes right.*

\- Gary Ridgway "

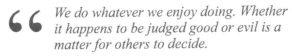

We do whatever we enjoy doing. Whether it happens to be judged good or evil is a matter for others to decide.

- Ian Brady

Satan gets into people and makes them do things they don't want to.

- Herbert Mullin

For me a corpse has a beauty and dignity which a living body could never hold... There is a peace about death that soothes me.

- John Christie

Conclusion

They were good, nonviolent, innocent young people who did not deserve to die.

- David Maust

Conclusion

The facts within this book represent the depravity in the world. They represent the darkness that dwells among us, blending in with society. The people who, on the surface, look just like you and me.

However, the people within this book and the people who are out there in the world with the same inclinations and motivations represent only a very small segment of humankind. As a whole, the light outweighs the dark tenfold, and we cannot forget that.

The good in the world is a force much stronger than the evil. So as long as we who are good can spread kindness and love as far as our reach will allow us, then mankind will not only survive, it will flourish.

Other Titles

By J R Mayfield

THE ONES
WHO GOT AWAY
WHEN SERIAL KILLERS FAIL TO KILL

J.R. MAYFIELD

The Ones Who Got Away

Excerpt

On July 22, 1991, at around 18.00 Tracy Edwards was having drinks with friends when Dahmer approached the group. He claimed to be a photographer and asked if any of the group would like to make some extra money posing for nude photos. Edwards accepted the offer and they made their way back to Dahmer's apartment.

Upon entering the apartment Edwards noticed a terrible odour, but Dahmer explained it was a problem with a sewer pipe and assured Edwards that the landlord was working to get it fixed promptly. Dahmer sat Edwards down, and at one point diverted Edwards' attention to the fish tank.

As Edwards turned to look, Dahmer snapped a handcuff onto his left wrist and unsuccessfully attempted to cuff the other wrist. Edwards was already confused, but Dahmer faked that it was all for the shoot and led Edwards toward the bedroom. In the bedroom 'The Exorcist 3' was playing on the TV, and Edwards noticed a foul smell coming from a blue drum in the room. When he turned back to Dahmer, he noticed he was now brandishing a knife, explaining how he intended to take nude photos of Edwards.

Dahmer began chanting indecipherable words, then he asked Edwards to lay face down on the bed with his hands behind his back, but Edwards laid on his side so Dahmer couldn't cuff his other hand. Then Dahmer laid his head on Edwards' chest listening to his heartbeat and told Edwards how he was going to eat his heart.

In order to reason with Dahmer, and possibly buy some time, Edwards agreed to pose for photos if they could head back into the front room, to which Dahmer agreed, and they then went and sat back on the couch, where Dahmer continued to rock and chant and pay Edwards little attention.

Edwards then asked to use the bathroom, and when he stood up Dahmer didn't, nor was Dahmer holding the other handcuff. Edwards realised this was his best chance to get out, he punched Dahmer in the face and ran, he made it out of the apartment building, where he managed to flag down a passing police car. The police officers listened to Edwards' story and went to check out Dahmer, who explained that it was all a big misunderstanding, which the police officers may have almost believed until they saw polaroids of dismembered bodies. Dahmer was subdued, and the officers called for backup.

Upon searching Dahmer's apartment officers found a plethora of horrific discoveries, coming across everything from severed heads in the fridge, to preserved penises, and severed hands to whole skeletons. When interrogated Dahmer confessed to everything, giving gruesome details into all the murders, and even identifying the victims. Dahmer received 16 consecutive life sentences in total in 1992 but served just over 2 years before an inmate beat him to death in November 1994 for bragging about his crimes.

Tracy Edwards' ordeal was over, he had managed to escape one of the most prolific serial killers America has ever known. Not only had he accomplished this, but a real-life monster had been caught and brought to justice all thanks to this man. Which is why it is all the more regrettable that unlike the other survivors in this book, who went on to become motivational speakers and advocates for certain causes, Edwards did not.

In 2011 Edwards, whilst living on the streets, became involved in the drowning death of another homeless man, and in 2012 he was sentenced to one and a half years in prison, along with two years extended supervision for aiding a felon which was reduced from first-degree recklessly endangering safety thanks to a plea deal.

Buy 'The Ones Who Got Away" on Amazon now!

About The Author

J. R. Mayfield: Author by day, masked crime fighter by night (this may or may not be true). He has an unhealthy obsession with all things grim, macabre, unearthly, and shocking. He loves to discuss and write about true crime and other topics such as the supernatural, extraterrestrial life, and urban legends. He is the founder and owner of **Human Cattle,** a media company specialising in the dark side of humanity and beyond. If you would like to know more you can visit the Human Cattle website or follow us on the following social media platforms.

www.facebook.com/cattlehuman
www.twitter.com/human_cattle
www.humancattle.com

Want More?

To keep up-to-date with new book releases, blog posts, videos and more, visit our website now!

www.humancattle.com

Thank you for reading!

Printed in Great Britain
by Amazon